In the Dog Kitchen

Great Snack Recipes for Your Dog

JULIE VAN ROSENDAAL

TOUCHWOOD EDITIONS

Library and Archives Canada Cataloguing in Publication
Van Rosendaal, Julie, 1970-
In the dog kitchen : great snack recipes for your dog / Julie Van Rosendaal.

ISBN 1-894739-07-8

1. Dogs--Food--Recipes. I. Title.

SF427.4.V35 2005   636.7'0855   C2005-902172-1

Front cover image: *Sidney*, Ruth Linka
Back cover image: *Julie Van Rosendaal with Cricket*, Mike Semenchuk
-Interior images: istockphoto.com unless otherwise indicated.

Every effort has been made to obtain permission for the photographs used in this book. If there is an omission or error the author and publisher would be grateful to be so informed.

TouchWood Editions acknowledges the financial support for its publishing program from the Government of Canada through the Book Publishing Industry Development Program (BPIDP), Canada Council for the Arts, and the province of British Columbia through the British Columbia Arts Council.

TouchWood Editions	TouchWood Editions
#108-17665 66A Avenue	PO Box 468
Surrey, BC V3S 2A7	Custer, WA
www.touchwoodeditions.com	98240-0468

BRITISH COLUMBIA ARTS COUNCIL
Supported by the Province of British Columbia

Canada Council for the Arts

Conseil des Arts du Canada

2   3   4   5   08 07

PRINTED AND BOUND IN CANADA

for Buddah

Anne reading to Sundance

Table of Contents

Sugs

Introduction

Someone once said "my goal in life is to be as good a person as my dog already thinks I am." We see each other through our friends' eyes. When our friends are dogs, it's no surprise they make us feel on top of the world. As Ann Landers noted, it's easy to accept such admiration as conclusive evidence that we are wonderful.

Our dogs give us everything they have, and its nice once in awhile to be able to repay their unconditional kindness with a batch of freshly baked cookies, without all the additives and preservatives of the store-bought kind. Dogs are infinitely more grateful and enthusiastic than any human for culinary endeavors made on their behalf. Unlike a person, a dog will love you forever for the price of a cheese biscuit.

What your dog eats is mainly up to you, but partly up to him; their tastes and needs vary as much as ours do, depending on their size, health, activity level and what they like to eat. Most dogs adore cheese, peanut butter and meat, and probably wouldn't mind combining those flavors. Their tastes differ from ours in that they will most likely find a brownie made out of chicken hearts and spread with peanut butter quite palatable! It's important to note however that foods that are good for us don't necessarily make healthy choices for our dogs. Dogs have very different digestive systems and nutritional needs; the following pages will outline some common ingredients that are potentially harmful. All the goodies in this book are made from easy to find, human-grade ingredients that are safe for dogs to eat. Consult your vet if you're unsure of what choices to make for his daily diet.

Even though their ideas of what makes a cookie delicious differ greatly from ours, dogs love treats as much as the rest of us. But remember that just like people, dogs can overeat and gain weight if they indulge in too many snacks. Good nutrition is imperative for a long and healthy life.

I hope your dog enjoys these treats as much as my dog friends do! Don't be afraid to experiment with ingredients you know he likes. Healthy treats make great rewards when training your new puppy, and great gifts for all the dogs in your life. Enjoy!

What People Can Eat, But Dogs Can't

The recipes in this book use ingredients that are safe to feed dogs, although, like people's, dogs' tastes vary. When it comes to people food, there are many foods that can be harmful to dogs, even if they are good for us. It could be dangerous to feed your dogs table scraps if you don't know what they might react negatively to.

Here are some foods that can be toxic and potentially deadly to dogs:

Chocolate is the number one craving among humans. Dogs love it too, but for them it can be deadly. It contains theobromine, which, when ingested by a dog in sufficient quantities, acts as a cardiac stimulant, releasing adrenaline that causes the heart to race or beat irregularly. Signs of chocolate poisoning include vomiting, diarrhea, excessive urination, muscle tremors, and hyperactivity, followed by depression and in severe cases seizures, coma, and even death.

Cocoa powder and baking chocolate are the most toxic forms; dark chocolate contains nine times the theobromine of milk chocolate, and a few ounces can potentially kill a medium-sized dog. Milk chocolate has the least amount of theobromine, so it is the least harmful. If you discover your dog has eaten chocolate, consult your vet immediately. Carob chips and powder make excellent substitutes for chocolate in dog treats.

Coffee grounds or beans can cause symptoms similar to those of chocolate toxicity and can be just as serious.

Raisins, grapes, and related products such as juice and wine can also be harmful to canines. Many dogs love raisins, but these can cause kidney failure and even death if consumed in large quantities.

Onions contain thiosulphate, which can damage red blood cells and cause anemia if eaten regularly or in large quantities. Dogs lack the enzyme necessary to properly digest onions, so eating them can result in gas, vomiting, diarrhea, and general gastrointestinal distress. This goes for cooked and dehydrated onions and onion powder as well.

Garlic is in the onion family, but it is safe for your dog in small quantities provided it is not raw. You can use raw garlic in your cookies, but they must be baked in order for your dog to digest it properly. Fresh, dehydrated, and powdered garlic are safe for your dog in moderation. Some believe garlic acts as a flea repellant, but the latest research shows this to be a misconception.

Avocados have been reported to be toxic to dogs. Symptoms include difficulty breathing, abdominal enlargement, and abnormal fluid accumulation in the chest, abdomen, and sac around the heart.

Pits, stones, and seeds from apples, apricots, cherries, peaches, and plums can be toxic if ingested. Symptoms of toxicity include apprehension, dilated pupils, difficulty breathing, hyperventilation, and shock. Depending on the size of your dog, they also pose a choking hazard.

Macadamia nuts can be toxic even if only a few are consumed. Watch for symptoms such as weakness, depression, vomiting, muscle tremors, and lameness or stiffness.

Moldy or spoiled foods can cause food poisoning in animals as well as humans. Some pets can also develop tremors as a result of ingesting certain molds.

Nutmeg in high doses can be toxic, even fatal. Signs of toxicity include tremors, seizures, and other nervous system abnormalities.

Rhubarb leaves are toxic if your dog ingests them. Symptoms include staggering, trembling, breathing difficulties, weakness, diarrhea, and increased drinking and urinating.

Yeast dough will rise in the stomach if ingested, producing alcohol as it ferments. This will expand your dog's stomach uncomfortably and could lead to alcohol toxicity. Symptoms include vomiting, abdominal discomfort, bloating, lethargy, and depression.

Some advice about **milk**:

Vets have differing opinions about whether or not it's a good idea to feed your dog milk. Many dogs lack lactase, the enzyme required by their digestive system to break down the lactose in milk. This results in a lot of undigested sugar in a dog's intestinal tract, which can lead to vomiting and diarrhea. It's the same thing that happens to people who are lactose intolerant.

Although many dogs are lactose intolerant, some are not. Many dogs love milk and other dairy products and can eat them without suffering any gastrointestinal problems. If you aren't sure whether dairy products cause your dog discomfort, check with your veterinarian. Because the lactose in buttermilk has already been broken down, it can generally be consumed by those with lactose intolerance without it causing discomfort. Yogurt with active cultures, low-fat and non-fat milk, hard cheeses, and cottage cheese are also lower in lactose than regular milk. Stock or water can generally be substituted for milk called for in these recipes.

Some advice about **salt**:

As for all mammals, sodium, chloride, and potassium are essential for dogs' bodily functions and to prevent dehydration. Salt also enhances the flavours of the other ingredients in a recipe, making dog cookies taste better! Too much salt can be harmful, though, so keep amounts to a minimum. If you think your dog is getting enough salt in his diet from his regular food, omit it when you bake treats.

Food allergies and intolerances are common in dogs just as they are in humans. Food intolerances differ from actual allergies in that they most often result in gastrointestinal discomfort, diarrhea, or vomiting, and aren't as severe as real allergies. This often leads to conflicting reports and confusion surrounding some ingredients. Studies have shown that the most common ingredients to cause food allergies are beef, dairy products, chicken, wheat, chicken eggs, corn, and soy—the most common ingredients in manufactured dog food. The incidences of allergic reactions are believed to be associated with the amount of exposure to a particular food. In an effort to combat food allergies, there is an increase in dog foods made with lamb and rice, ingredients that previously weren't used in pet foods.

Abby

DROP COOKIES

Peanut Butter & Banana Cookies

These soft, cakey cookies are perfect for older dogs who have difficulty with harder biscuits. If you like, add a handful of carob chips or chopped peanuts.

Pork Chop

½ cup natural peanut butter
2 ripe bananas, mashed
1 egg
2 tbsp. honey
¾ cup milk or water
2 cups whole wheat flour
1 tsp. baking powder

Preheat oven to 350° F.

In a large bowl, combine peanut butter, bananas, egg, honey, and milk or water. Stir until well blended, but don't worry about getting all the lumps of banana out. Add flour and baking powder and stir just until combined.

Drop spoonfuls of dough onto a cookie sheet that has been sprayed with non-stick spray. Bake for about 15 minutes, until springy to the touch.

Makes about 2 dozen cookies. Store in a tightly sealed container or freeze.

"You can say any foolish thing to a dog, and the dog will give you a look that says, 'Wow, you're right! I never would've thought of that!'"

~Dave Barry

Oatmeal Carob Chip Cookies

This is the closest your dog will come to having real chocolate chip cookies. Remember that dogs don't appreciate them warm and gooey straight from the oven like we do—let these cool first so they don't burn their tongues.

2 cups whole wheat flour
½ cup oats
1 tsp. baking soda
½ cup milk or water
¼ cup canola oil
¼ cup honey
2 eggs
1 tsp. vanilla
½ cup carob chips

"I named my dog 'Stay', so I can say, 'Come here, Stay. Come here, Stay.'"
⌐Stephen Wright

4

Boris

Preheat oven to 350° F.

In a large bowl, combine flour, oats, and baking soda. In a medium bowl, stir together milk (or water), oil, honey, eggs, and vanilla. Add to the flour mixture along with the carob chips, and mix just until blended.

Drop large spoonfuls of dough 1" to 2" apart on a cookie sheet that has been sprayed with non-stick spray. Bake for about 15 minutes, until springy to the touch.

Makes about 2 dozen cookies. Store in a tightly sealed container.

Oatmeal, Banana & Carob Chip Cookies ~ Add a mashed ripe banana to the milk mixture; mix and bake as directed.

Chicken Cookies with Rice

Brown rice is the best cooked grain to feed your dog. It is a high-fibre complex carbohydrate, and unlike white rice it contains the extra nutrients found in the germ and outer layers of the grain. These cookies are soft and cakey, perfect for dogs who have difficulty chewing.

2 cups whole wheat flour
¼ cup skim milk powder
1 tsp. baking powder
Pinch salt
½ cup chicken broth or water
1 jar baby food chicken stew
1 egg
2 tbsp. canola oil
2 tbsp. honey
1 cup cooked rice, cooled
½ cup shredded cooked chicken or turkey

"To err is human; to forgive, canine."
~Anonymous

Preheat oven to 350° F.

In a large bowl, combine flour, skim milk powder, baking powder, and salt. In a small bowl, stir together broth or water, baby food, egg, oil, and honey. Add to the dry ingredients along with the rice and chicken, and stir just until blended.

Drop spoonfuls of dough onto a cookie sheet that has been sprayed with non-stick spray. Bake for about 20 minutes, until springy to the touch. Let them cool on the cookie sheet.

Makes about 2 dozen cookies. Store in a tightly covered container in the fridge, or freeze.

Daisy

Leftovers Cookies

These are perfect treats to make with the remnants of a big turkey dinner. They have just enough batter to bind together whatever meat and veggies you have around. Dogs need to celebrate too!

1 cup mashed potatoes, cooled
½ – 1 cup chopped cooked chicken, beef, or pork
½ cup cooked carrots, chopped or mashed
½ cup chicken or beef broth
1 egg
2 tbsp. canola oil
1 clove garlic, crushed
2 cups whole wheat flour
½ cup cornmeal
1 tsp. baking powder
Pinch salt

"If a dog will not come to you after having looked you in the face, you should go home and examine your conscience."
~Woodrow Wilson

Preheat oven to 350° F.

In a large bowl, combine mashed potatoes, meat, carrots, broth, egg, oil, and garlic. Add flour, cornmeal, baking powder, and salt, and stir just until blended.

Drop large spoonfuls of dough onto a cookie sheet that has been sprayed with non-stick spray, or use your fingers to shape it into balls. Press each cookie down to flatten a little with your hand. Bake for about 20 minutes, until springy to the touch. Cool on the cookie sheet or transfer to a wire rack.

Makes about 2 dozen cookies. Store extras in a tightly sealed container in the fridge, or freeze.

Dog Food Cookies

Okay, these will stink a bit while they're baking if you're not a dog, but if you are, you will go crazy for them.

Ceilidh

2 cups whole wheat flour
¼ cup skim milk powder
1 tsp. baking powder
½ tsp. garlic powder
Pinch salt
1 can (374 g) wet dog food, any flavour
½ cup water or broth
1 egg
1 tbsp. canola oil
1 tbsp. honey

Preheat oven to 350° F.

In a large bowl, combine flour, skim milk powder, baking powder, garlic powder, and salt. In a medium bowl, stir together dog food, water, egg, oil, and honey. Add to the flour mixture and stir until well blended.

Drop spoonfuls of dough onto a cookie sheet that has been sprayed with non-stick spray, and flatten each cookie a little with your hand. If you like, add more flour to make a firmer dough, roll into balls, and flatten with the bottom of a glass.

Bake for about 20 minutes, until firm and springy to the touch.

Makes about 2 dozen cookies. Store extras in a tightly sealed container in the fridge, or freeze.

"Acquiring a dog may be the only time a person gets to choose a relative."
~Unknown

Chicken & Cheese Drop Biscuits

I always use aged cheddar cheese when I bake, because it has much more flavour. If you like, stir in some chopped sun-dried tomatoes or bits of chopped leftover chicken or ham. You may love these as much as your dog does! Just don't let him see you eating them or he may learn to beg for people food.

2 cups whole wheat flour
1 tbsp. baking powder
2 tsp. dried parsley flakes or basil (optional)
¼ tsp. garlic powder
Pinch salt
½ – 1 cup grated cheddar cheese
¾ cup chicken stock
2 tbsp. canola oil

"If you get to thinkin' you're a person of some influence,
try orderin' someone else's dog around!"
~Conventional cowboy wisdom

Preheat oven to 400° F.

In a large bowl, combine flour, baking powder, parsley, garlic powder, and salt. Stir in the cheese. Add chicken stock and oil, and stir just until blended.

Drop heaping spoonfuls of dough onto a cookie sheet that has been sprayed with non-stick spray. If you prefer, pat the dough about ½" thick on a lightly floured surface and cut into biscuits with a cookie cutter or knife.

Echo

Bake for about 15 minutes, until golden. Cool on the cookie sheet or transfer to a wire rack.

Makes about 2 dozen biscuits. Store in a tightly sealed container, or freeze.

Maple Apple Walnut Hermits

Walnuts are particularly high in vitamin E, an antioxidant that helps with circulation, reproduction, and immune system function.

2 cups whole wheat flour
1 tsp. baking soda
¼ tsp. cinnamon
Pinch salt
¾ cup milk or water
2 tbsp. maple syrup or honey
2 tbsp. canola oil
1 egg
1 large apple, grated
½ cup chopped walnuts

"The greatest pleasure of a dog is that you may make a fool of yourself with him, and not only will he not scold you, but he will make a fool of himself, too."
~Samuel Butler

Preheat oven to 350° F.

In a large bowl, combine flour, baking soda, cinnamon, and salt. In a small bowl, stir together milk, maple syrup, oil, and egg. Add to the flour mixture along with the grated apple and walnuts, and stir just until blended.

Drop spoonfuls of dough onto a cookie sheet that has been sprayed with non-stick spray. Bake for about 20 minutes, until springy to the touch. Cool on the cookie sheet or transfer to a wire rack.

Makes about 2 dozen cookies. Store in a tightly sealed container, or freeze.

Apple & Cheddar Hermits ~ Substitute ½ cup grated cheddar cheese for the walnuts, or add both! Mix and bake as directed.

Carrot Pumpkin Hermits

The double whammy of pumpkin and carrots delivers a high dose of vitamin A in the form of beta carotene. Vitamin A is particularly important for growing puppies, who aren't yet capable of liver storage of this vitamin.

2 cups whole wheat flour
1 tsp. baking soda
½ tsp. cinnamon
1 cup canned pure pumpkin (not pie filling)
½ cup water
2 tbsp. canola oil
2 tbsp. molasses
1 egg
1 large carrot, grated

"A dog is the only thing on earth that loves you more than he loves himself."
~Josh Billings

Preheat oven to 350° F.

In a large bowl, combine flour, baking soda, and cinnamon. In a medium bowl, stir together pumpkin, water, oil, molasses, and egg. Add to the dry ingredients along with the grated carrot, and stir just until blended.

Julie

Drop spoonfuls of dough onto a cookie sheet that has been sprayed with non-stick spray. Bake for about 20 minutes, until springy to the touch. Cool on the cookie sheet or transfer to a wire rack.

Makes about 2 dozen cookies. Store in a tightly sealed container, or freeze.

Sweet Potato Hermits ~ Substitute cooked, mashed sweet potato for the pumpkin. Mix and bake as directed.

Pumpkin Apple Hermits ~ Substitute one unpeeled, grated apple for the grated carrot. Mix and bake as directed.

Sweet Potato, Oatmeal & Cottage Cheese Drops

Cottage cheese and oats are both great sources of protein, calcium, and vitamin B12. The potato adds sweetness, additional fibre, and vitamins and minerals such as beta carotene.

1½ cups whole wheat flour
2 cups quick oats
1 tsp. baking powder
½ tsp. cinnamon (optional)
½ cup water or milk
2 tbsp. molasses or honey
2 tbsp. canola oil
1 egg
1 cup mashed sweet potato (about 1 medium potato) or
        canned pure pumpkin
1 cup cottage cheese

"To his dog, every man is King; hence the constant popularity of dogs."
~Aldous Huxley

Preheat oven to 350° F.

In a large bowl, combine flour, oats, baking powder, and cinnamon. In a small bowl, stir together water, molasses, oil, and egg. Add to the flour mixture along with the mashed sweet potato and cottage cheese, and stir until well blended.

Drop spoonfuls of dough onto a cookie sheet that has been sprayed with non-stick spray. Bake for about 20 minutes, until springy to the touch. Cool on the cookie sheet or transfer to a wire rack.

Makes about 2½ dozen cookies. Store extras in a tightly sealed container, or freeze.

Guinness

ROLLED COOKIES

Applesauce Oat Strips ⁓ 22

Milk Bones with Wheat Germ & Honey ⁓ 24

Flaxseed & Molasses Sticks ⁓ 26

Beef Bones ⁓ 28

Beef & Cheese Bones ⁓ 29

Chicken or Turkey Bones ⁓ 29

Peanut Butter Bones ⁓ 30

Peanut Butter & Cream Cheese Sandwich Cookies ⁓ 32

Chicken Liver Cookies ⁓ 34

Gingerbread Mailmen ⁓ 36

Leftover Turkey & Rosemary Treats ⁓ 38

Dalmatians ⁓ 40

Parmesan, Cornmeal & Sun-Dried Tomato Biscuits ⁓ 42

Puppy Pizzas ⁓ 44

Cheese Slices ⁓ 46

Cheddar Sesame Crackers ⁓ 48

Bacon Cheddar Crackers ⁓ 49

Tomato Basil Wheat Thins ⁓ 50

Oatmeal Cookies with Peaches & Molasses ⁓ 52

Applesauce Oat Strips

If you don't have applesauce, peel and chop an apple and microwave it in a small dish with some water, then mash it with a fork.

Kona

JANET & RICK HUGHES

2 cups whole wheat flour
1 cup oats
1 tsp. cinnamon
½ cup applesauce
¼ cup water
1 egg
1 tbsp. molasses or honey

Preheat oven to 350° F.

In a large bowl, combine flour, oats, and cinnamon. In a small bowl, stir together applesauce, water, egg, and molasses.

Add the applesauce mixture to the flour mixture and stir until well blended. On a lightly floured surface, roll the dough out about ½" thick and cut into 1" x 3" strips with a pastry cutter, pizza wheel, or knife.

Transfer to a cookie sheet that has been sprayed with non-stick spray and bake for about 20 minutes, until golden and firm. Let them cool on the cookie sheet, or turn the oven off but leave them inside for several hours to harden as they cool.

Makes about 3 dozen cookies. Store in a tightly sealed container, or freeze.

"There is no psychiatrist in the world like a puppy licking your face."
~Ben Williams

Milk Bones with
Wheat Germ & Honey

Here's a classic recipe that keeps well and which dogs adore. A batch of these wrapped in cellophane and tied with ribbon makes a great (and inexpensive!) gift for your favourite pooch. If you have a donut cutter, try cutting these into rings, then loop a ribbon through a whole bunch.

Kona

2 cups whole wheat flour
½ cup wheat germ
¼ cup skim milk powder
Pinch salt
½ cup chicken stock or water
¼ cup canola oil
1 egg
1 tbsp. honey or molasses

"My goal in life is to be as good a person as my dog already thinks I am."
~Unknown

Preheat oven to 350° F.

In a large bowl, combine flour, wheat germ, skim milk powder, and salt. In a small bowl, stir together stock, oil, egg, and honey. If you want, crumble the eggshell into the dry ingredients. Add the wet ingredients to the dry ingredients and stir until well blended.

Gently knead the dough a few times on a lightly floured surface, then roll it out ¼"–½" thick. Cut into desired shapes with a cookie cutter or knife, and transfer to an ungreased cookie sheet. Prick each cookie a few times with a fork.

Bake for about 20 minutes, depending on the size and thickness of the cookies, until pale golden and firm. Turn the oven off but leave them inside for a few hours to harden as they cool.

Makes about 3 dozen cookies. Store in a tightly sealed container.

Flaxseed & Molasses Sticks

Harder biscuits keep better than softer ones—let these cool and harden in the oven if you want your stash to last a long time.

2 cups whole wheat flour
¼ cup ground flaxseed
1 tsp. baking soda
½ tsp. cinnamon
¼ cup canola oil
¼ cup dark molasses
¼ cup water

Preheat oven to 350° F.

In a large bowl, combine flour, flaxseed, baking soda, and cinnamon. In a small bowl, stir together oil, molasses, and water. Add to the flour mixture and stir until you have a soft dough.

On a lightly floured surface, roll the dough out about ½" thick. Cut into strips ½" x 3" with a knife. Transfer to an ungreased cookie sheet and bake for about 20 minutes, until firm. Let them cool on the cookie sheet, or turn the oven off but leave them inside for several hours to harden as they cool.

Makes about 2 dozen cookies. Store in a tightly sealed container.

"Did you ever walk into a room and forget why you walked in?
I think that is how dogs spend their lives."
~ Sue Murphy

Beef Bones

Many people give their dogs bones as a treat, but this isn't necessarily a good idea; splintered bones can get caught in the digestive tract and potentially tear the surrounding tissue. If you do give your dog a bone, it's a good idea to first submerge it in boiling water for a minute to kill surface bacteria, then let it cool. And don't leave the dog alone with it, unless it's one of these.

1 cup lean ground beef
1 clove garlic, crushed
2 cups whole wheat flour
1 cup cornmeal
¾ cup beef stock, tomato juice, or water
¼ cup canola oil
1 egg

"The one absolutely unselfish friend that man can have in this selfish world, the one that never deserts him, the one that never proves ungrateful or treacherous, is his dog."
~George Graham

Preheat oven to 350° F.

Over medium heat, cook ground beef with garlic in a skillet until no longer pink; drain any excess fat and set aside to cool.

In a large bowl, combine flour, cornmeal, and ground beef. In a small bowl, stir together beef stock, oil, and egg. Add to the dry ingredients and mix until thoroughly blended.

Sprout

On a lightly floured surface, roll dough about ½" thick and cut into 1" x 3" strips with a knife. Place on an ungreased cookie sheet and bake for about 30 minutes, until firm. Let them cool on the cookie sheet.

Makes about 3 dozen cookies. Store in a sealed container in the fridge, or freeze.

Beef & Cheese Bones ~ Add ½ cup grated cheddar cheese along with the beef. Mix and bake as directed.

Chicken or Turkey Bones ~ Substitute ground chicken or turkey for the beef, and use chicken stock instead of beef stock.

Peanut Butter Bones

This is one of my most popular recipes—dogs do backflips for them! Use regular or chunky peanut butter and make them as big or small as you like, according to the size of your dog.

JULIE VAN ROSENDAAL

Buddah

2½ cups whole wheat flour
½ cup oatmeal
½ cup chopped peanuts (optional)
1 tsp. baking powder
1 cup natural peanut butter
1 cup skim milk or water
2 tbsp. honey

Preheat oven to 350° F.

In a large bowl, combine flour, oatmeal, peanuts, and baking powder. Add peanut butter, milk, and honey, and stir until you have a stiff dough. Use your hands if you need to at the end in order to blend it well.

On a lightly floured surface, roll or pat the dough out about ½" thick. Cut into 1" x 3" strips with a knife and place on an ungreased cookie sheet.

Bake for about 20 minutes, until golden. Let them cool on the cookie sheet, or turn the oven off but leave them inside for several hours to harden as they cool.

Makes about 2 dozen bones. Store in a tightly sealed container.

"Anybody who doesn't know what soap tastes like never washed a dog."
~Franklin P. Jones

Peanut Butter & Cream Cheese Sandwich Cookies

These cookies are absolutely adorable. If you are baking them for a friend, pack them in a Chinese takeout container lined with tissue.

Cookies:
2 cups whole wheat flour
½ cup cornmeal
1 egg
½ cup natural peanut butter
1½ cups water

Filling:
4 oz. (125 g) light cream cheese
¼ cup natural peanut butter (optional)
1 tbsp. honey (optional)

"No matter how little money and how few possessions you own, having a dog makes you rich."
~Louis Sabin

Preheat oven to 350° F.

In a large bowl, combine flour, cornmeal, egg, peanut butter, and water, and stir until you have a soft dough. On a lightly

Echo & Kona

floured surface, roll the dough out about ¼" thick and cut into small circles with a cookie cutter or glass rim.

Place on an ungreased cookie sheet and prick a few times with a fork to keep them from puffing up. Bake for about 15 minutes, until pale golden and firm. Cool completely on the cookie sheet.

In a small bowl, beat cream cheese, peanut butter, and honey until smooth. Spread the filling on half of the cooled cookies and top each one with a second cookie. (If you like, you can forego the peanut butter and honey and spread them with plain cream cheese.)

Makes about 2½ dozen cookies. Store in a tightly covered container in the fridge.

Chicken Liver Cookies

Dogs require much more protein than humans, and organ meat is one of the best sources. Chicken livers, and often chicken hearts, are inexpensive and easy to find at the grocery store. Heart is particularly low in fat.

2½ cups whole wheat flour
½ cup cornmeal
¼ cup grated Parmesan cheese (optional)
1 cup raw chicken livers or hearts
¼ cup water or chicken stock
2 tbsp. canola oil
1 egg

"A dog is one of the remaining reasons why some people can be persuaded to go for a walk."
~ O. A.

Preheat oven to 350° F.

In a large bowl, combine flour, cornmeal, and Parmesan cheese. In the bowl of a food processor, whiz chicken livers, water, oil, and egg until well blended. Don't worry about getting all the small lumps out.

Add the liver mixture to the flour mixture and stir just until combined, adding a little extra flour if necessary to make a soft dough.

On a well-floured surface, roll the dough out ¼"–½" thick. Cut into desired shapes with a cookie cutter, glass rim, or knife, and transfer to a cookie sheet that has been sprayed with non-stick spray.

Bake for about 20 minutes, until firm. Let them cool on the cookie sheet, or turn the oven off and leave them inside for several hours to harden as they cool.

Makes about 3 dozen cookies. Store in a tightly covered container in the fridge, or freeze.

Gingerbread Mailmen

These make a great gift, especially during the holidays. You can press in some carob chips or peanuts for eyes before you bake them—but avoid using raisins, which can be toxic to dogs.

2 cups whole wheat flour
1 tsp. baking soda
½ tsp. each cinnamon and ground ginger
¼ cup canola oil
¼ cup dark molasses
¼ cup water

Madges

Preheat oven to 350° F.

In a large bowl, combine flour, baking soda, cinnamon, and ginger. In a small bowl, stir together oil, molasses, and water. Add to the dry ingredients and stir just until you have a soft dough.

On a lightly floured surface, roll the dough out about ¼" thick. Cut into gingerbread men or any other shape you like with a cookie cutter, glass rim, or knife. Transfer to an ungreased cookie sheet.

Bake for about 15 minutes, until firm. Let them cool on the cookie sheet, or turn the oven off and leave them inside for several hours to harden as they cool.

Makes about 2½ dozen cookies. Store in a tightly covered container.

"A dog is not 'almost human,' and I know of no greater insult to the canine race than to describe it as such."
~John Holmes

Leftover Turkey & Rosemary Treats

This is a great way to use up the very last of a roast chicken or turkey. I usually end up with flavourful turkey sludge in the bottom of the pot when I cook the carcass to make stock, and I use this to make these treats.

2 cups whole wheat flour
½ cup cornmeal
¼ cup grated Parmesan cheese
2 tbsp. chopped fresh rosemary, or 1 tbsp. dried
Pinch salt
1 cup meaty chicken stock (boil your chicken or turkey carcass until all the bits fall off)
1 egg
2 tbsp. canola oil
1 clove garlic, crushed

"A dog can express more with his tail in minutes than his owner can express with his tongue in hours."
~Anonymous

Preheat oven to 350° F.

In a large bowl, combine flour, cornmeal, Parmesan cheese, rosemary, and salt. In a small bowl, stir together chicken stock, eggs, oil, and garlic. Add to the dry ingredients and stir until well blended, adding a little extra flour if the dough is too sticky.

MayMay

On a lightly floured surface, roll or pat the dough about ½" thick and cut into shapes with a cookie cutter, glass rim, or knife. Transfer to an ungreased cookie sheet.

Bake for about 20 minutes, until golden and firm. Let them cool on the cookie sheet, or turn the oven off and leave them inside for several hours to harden as they cool.

Makes about 2 dozen cookies. Store in a tightly sealed container, or freeze.

Dalmatians

Don't be surprised if your dog figures out how to open these up and lick off the filling first! If you don't have cream cheese, leave it out and cut the dough into any shape biscuits you like.

Cookies:
1½ cups whole wheat flour
¼ cup carob powder
½ tsp. baking soda
Pinch salt
¼ cup canola oil
¼ cup dark molasses
¼ cup water

Filling:
4 oz. (125 g) spreadable light cream cheese

"Dogs are not our whole life, but they make our lives whole."
~Roger Caras

Preheat oven to 350° F.

In a large bowl, combine flour, carob powder, baking soda, and salt. In a small bowl, stir together oil, molasses, and water. Add to the dry ingredients and stir just until you have a soft dough.

On a lightly floured surface, roll the dough out about ¼" thick. Cut into small rounds with a cookie cutter or glass rim. Transfer to an ungreased cookie sheet.

Bake for about 15 minutes, until golden around the edges and firm. Let them cool on the cookie sheet, or turn the oven off and leave them inside for several hours to harden as they cool.

Once the cookies have cooled completely, spread half of them with cream cheese and top each one with a second cookie to make sandwiches.

Makes about 1½ dozen cookies. Store in a tightly covered container in the fridge.

Parmesan, Cornmeal & Sun Dried Tomato Biscuits

Some dogs are lactose intolerant—they lack the enzyme required to properly digest lactose. This affects some pets more than others and can cause gas or diarrhea. Dogs who cannot digest milk can normally digest yogurt with active cultures. Since the lactose in buttermilk has already been broken down, it can be substituted for the yogurt.

2 cups whole wheat flour
½ cup cornmeal
¼ cup grated Parmesan cheese
1 tsp. baking powder
Pinch salt
1 cup plain yogurt, thinned with a little water if it's really thick
¼ cup sun-dried tomatoes (packed in oil or soaked in water),
    drained and chopped
1 egg
1 clove garlic, crushed

Preheat oven to 400° F.

In a large bowl, combine flour, cornmeal, Parmesan cheese, baking powder, and salt. In a small bowl, stir together yogurt, tomatoes, egg, and garlic. Add to the dry ingredients and stir until well blended.

On a lightly floured surface, pat the dough out about ½" thick. Cut into small rounds with a biscuit cutter or glass rim, or into squares with a knife. Transfer to an ungreased baking sheet and bake for about 20 minutes, until golden.

Makes about 2 dozen 2" biscuits. Store in a tightly sealed container, or freeze.

Puppy Pizzas

Olive and canola oils are healthy fats that contribute to a lush coat, clear skin, increased energy, and good muscle tone. The tomato paste in this recipe is a concentrated source of vitamin C. And how cute are teeny little pizzas for your dog? They can be topped with cooked ground beef as well if you like.

Crust:
2 cups whole wheat flour
1 tsp. baking powder
½ cup water
¼ cup olive or canola oil
1 egg

Topping:
1 small can tomato paste
1 clove garlic, crushed (optional)
½ tsp. dried oregano or Italian seasoning
¼ cup grated Parmesan cheese

"I can train any dog in five minutes. It's training the owner that takes longer."
~Barbara Woodhouse

Preheat oven to 350° F.

In a large bowl, combine flour and baking powder. In a small bowl, stir together water, oil, and egg; add to the flour mixture and stir until you have a soft dough. Add a little extra flour if it's too sticky.

On a smooth surface lightly sprinkled with flour or cornmeal, roll the dough out about ¼" thick. Cut into small rounds with a cookie cutter, glass rim, or knife, and transfer to an ungreased cookie sheet.

In a small bowl, stir together the tomato paste, garlic, and oregano. Spread over the dough rounds and sprinkle with Parmesan cheese.

Bake for about 15 minutes, until puffed and pale golden around the edges.

Makes about 3½ dozen 1½" pizzas. Store in a tightly sealed container in the fridge, or freeze.

Cheese Slices

Despite common belief, neither garlic nor brewer's yeast will do much to repel fleas. Many dogs like the taste of both though—just make sure you don't feed them raw garlic, which is difficult to digest. Not to mention the breath . . .

2 cups whole wheat flour
½ cup oatmeal
¼ cup skim milk powder
½ cup grated cheddar cheese
¼ cup grated Parmesan cheese
¼ cup canola oil
⅓ cup water
1 egg
1 clove garlic, crushed

"No one appreciates the very special genius of your conversation as the dog does."
~Christopher Morley

Preheat oven to 350° F.

In a large bowl, combine flour, oatmeal, skim milk powder, and cheddar and Parmesan cheese. Add oil, water, egg, and garlic, and stir until you have a stiff dough. You may have to use your hands!

Vinni & Nelson

On a lightly floured surface, roll the dough out ¼"–½" thick. Cut into desired shapes with a cookie cutter or glass rim and place on an ungreased cookie sheet.

Bake for about 20 minutes, until golden. Let them cool on the cookie sheet, or turn the oven off and leave them inside for several hours to harden as they cool.

Makes about 2 dozen cookies. Store extras in a tightly sealed container.

Cheddar Sesame Crackers

Here are some treats you can share with your dog! Dip yours in antipasto and his in peanut butter. Don't let him see, or he may come to expect you to share your food.

1 cup whole wheat flour
½ cup grated cheddar cheese
Pinch salt
2 tbsp. canola oil
¼ cup chicken stock or water
Sesame seeds for sprinkling

Preheat oven to 375° F.

Combine the flour, cheese, and salt in the bowl of a food processor and pulse until well blended. Add the oil and pulse again. (If you don't have a food processor use a fork or whisk in a regular bowl.) Add the stock or water, and pulse or mix until it looks well blended and crumbly.

Turn the mixture out onto a lightly floured surface and gather it into a ball. Roll the dough out about ¼" thick. Sprinkle with sesame seeds and roll again lightly to help them adhere. Cut into 1" squares, rectangles, or whatever shape you like with a cookie cutter or knife.

Place on an ungreased cookie sheet, prick each cracker with a fork, and bake for about 20 minutes, until golden. Let them cool on the cookie sheet, or turn the oven off and leave them inside for several hours to harden as they cool.

Makes about 3 dozen crackers. Store in a tightly sealed container.

Bacon Cheddar Crackers ~ This is a great way to use up bacon drippings—scrape them from the pan (including all the bits!) into the food processor in place of the canola oil.

Tomato Basil Wheat Thins

These treats are perfect for small dogs, because they are so thin and can be cut as tiny as you like. Just make sure when you cut them out that they don't have sharp edges. If they're round, make sure that they aren't the same size as your dog's esophagus, or he may choke if they aren't chewed properly.

3 cups whole wheat flour
2 tsp. dried basil
Pinch salt
1 cup tomato juice
¼ cup canola oil

"Yesterday I was a dog. Today I'm a dog. Tomorrow I'll probably still be a dog. Sigh! There's so little hope for advancement."
~Snoopy

In a medium bowl, stir together flour, basil, and salt. Add tomato juice and oil and mix until you have a soft dough. Let the dough rest for about 15 minutes.

Preheat oven to 350° F.

Divide the dough in half. On a lightly floured surface, roll out one piece at a time into a rectangle that is about ⅛" thick. Place each whole piece of rolled-out dough on an ungreased baking sheet and cut into squares with a pizza wheel or knife, without separating the pieces. Prick each piece with a fork.

Bake for about 20 minutes, until firm.

Makes about 6 dozen cookies. Store in a tightly covered container.

Oatmeal Cookies with
Peaches & Molasses

If you have a donut cutter, cut ring-shaped cookies out of the dough. To give them as gifts, string several onto a nice ribbon, perhaps with a copy of this recipe!

3 cups oats, old-fashioned or quick-cooking
1 large peach or nectarine, peeled and sliced or chopped
1 egg
2 tbsp. canola oil
2 tbsp. molasses or honey
2 cups whole wheat flour
¼ tsp. cinnamon (optional)

Place the oats in a large bowl and pour a cup of water overtop. Let them stand for about 10 minutes. Preheat the oven to 350° F.

Place the peaches in a food processor along with about ¼ cup water and pulse until finely pureed. Add the egg, oil and molasses and pulse until well blended. Pour over the oats and stir until well blended. Add the flour and stir just until you have a stiff dough.

On a lightly floured surface, roll the dough out about ⅛" thick and cut into squares or other shapes with a cookie cutter or knife.

Transfer to an ungreased cookie sheet and bake for about 20 minutes, until firm. Turn the oven off, but leave the cookies inside to cool and harden.

Makes about 3 dozen cookies. Store extras in a tightly sealed container.

"I think dogs are the most amazing creatures; they give unconditional love. For me they are the role model for being alive."
~Gilda Radner

SHAPED COOKIES

Buttermilk Bagels

Make these even better by adding a handful of grated cheese, fresh chopped herbs, or some leftover cooked chicken or beef.

2 cups whole wheat flour
1 tsp. baking powder
½ tsp. baking soda
Pinch salt
1 cup buttermilk or thin plain yogurt
1 egg
1 tbsp. honey
Oats (for rolling)

Magnum

"The reason a dog has so many friends is that he wags his tail instead of his tongue."
~Anonymous

Preheat oven to 375° F.

In a large bowl, combine flour, baking powder, baking soda, and salt. In a medium bowl, stir together buttermilk, egg, and honey. Add to the dry ingredients, along with any additions you like, and stir until you have a soft ball of dough.

Knead the dough about 10 times on a well-floured surface. Pinch off small balls of dough (marble to walnut-sized) and roll them in oats to coat; poke your finger through the middle of the ball and shape the dough into a bagel. Place on a cookie sheet that has been sprayed with non-stick spray.

Bake for about 15 minutes, until golden and firm. Let the bagels cool on the cookie sheet, or turn the oven off but leave them inside for a few hours to harden as they cool.

Makes about 2 dozen bagels. Store in a tightly covered container, or freeze.

Peanut Butter Bagels ~ Stir ¼ cup natural peanut butter into buttermilk mixture. Mix and bake as directed, adding a little extra flour if the dough is too sticky.

Cinnamon Bun Bites

If you want to make more authentic-looking mini cinnamon buns for your dog, slice these a little thicker, bake as directed, and drizzle with cream cheese that has been thinned with a little honey and water. Drizzling is easy if you put the icing in a zip-lock bag and snip a teeny bit off one corner to squeeze it out.

2 cups whole wheat flour
1 tsp. baking powder
Pinch salt
½ cup water or milk
¼ cup canola oil
1 egg
1–2 tbsp. honey
1 tsp. cinnamon
¼ cup finely chopped walnuts or pecans (optional)
Light cream cheese for spreading (optional)

"It's no coincidence that man's best friend cannot talk."
~Anonymous

Preheat oven to 350° F.

In a large bowl, combine flour, baking powder, and salt. In a small bowl, stir together water, oil, and egg. Add to the dry ingredients and stir just until you have a soft dough.

On a lightly floured surface, roll or pat the dough into a rectangle that measures roughly 8" x 14". Drizzle with honey and sprinkle with cinnamon and nuts, if using. Starting from a long edge, roll the dough up jelly-role style and pinch the edge to seal. Using a sharp serrated knife or dental floss, slice ½" thick pieces and place slices cut side down on a cookie sheet that has been sprayed with non-stick spray.

Bake for about 15 minutes, until springy to the touch. Wait until they have cooled completely before you spread them with cream cheese.

Makes about 2 dozen cinnamon buns. Store in a tightly covered container, or freeze. If they are frosted, store the container in the fridge.

Cottage Cheese Corn Dogs

Cottage cheese is a great source of protein and B vitamins, as are organ meats and sardines. Try stirring some blueberries or chopped chicken liver into the muffin batter before baking.

2 cups whole wheat flour
1 cup cornmeal
2 tsp. baking powder
1 cup cottage cheese
1 cup chicken stock or buttermilk
1 egg

"Dogs have given us their absolute all. We are the centre of their universe, we are the focus of their love and faith and trust. They serve us in return for scraps. It is without a doubt the best deal man has ever made."
~Roger Caras

Preheat oven to 350° F.

In a large bowl, combine flour, cornmeal, and baking powder. In a small bowl, stir together cottage cheese, chicken stock, and egg. Add to the dry ingredients and stir just until blended.

Coat mini muffin tins with non-stick spray and fill them with batter. Bake for about 20 minutes, until springy to the touch. Remove from the pan and cool on a wire rack.

Makes 2½–3 dozen mini muffins. Store in a tightly sealed container, or freeze.

Tuna Sandwiches

These are deliciously fishy cookies with or without the cream cheese filling. Oily fish are rich in vitamin D, which aids in the absorption of calcium and contributes to healthy bones and teeth.

Cookies:
1 can tuna, salmon, or sardines (packed in water, undrained)
½ cup water
¼ cup canola or olive oil
1 clove garlic, crushed (optional)
2 cups whole wheat flour
1 cup cornmeal
Pinch salt

Filling (optional)**:**
1-8oz. (250 g) container spreadable light cream cheese

"I wonder if other dogs think poodles are members of a weird religious cult."
~Rita Rudner

Preheat oven to 350° F.

In a food processor, combine undrained tuna, salmon, or sardines, with water, oil, and garlic. Pulse until well blended and relatively smooth. In a large bowl, combine flour, cornmeal, and salt. Add the tuna mixture to the flour mixture and stir until you have a soft dough.

Roll the dough into walnut-sized balls and place on an ungreased cookie sheet. Press each one down once or twice (crisscrossed) with the back of a fork, like a peanut butter cookie.

Bake for about 15 minutes, until firm. Cool completely on the cookie sheet or on a wire rack.

To make sandwiches, spread half the cookies with cream cheese and top with a second cookie to make sandwiches.

Makes about 2 dozen cookies or 1 dozen sandwiches. Store in a tightly covered container in the fridge.

Crunchy Mint Cookies

If your buddy is going to have dog breath, it might as well be minty.

2 cups whole wheat flour
½ cup wheat germ, plus extra for rolling
¼ cup skim milk powder
¼ cup dried mint, or ½ cup chopped fresh mint
1 cup water
2 tbsp. canola oil

Max

Preheat oven to 350° F.

In a large bowl, combine flour, wheat germ, skim milk powder, and mint. Add water and oil and stir until you have a soft dough.

Roll the dough into walnut-sized balls, then roll the balls in wheat germ to coat. Place on a cookie sheet and flatten each cookie with a fork.

Bake for about 20 minutes, until firm. Turn off the oven but leave the cookies inside for several hours to harden as they cool.

Makes about 2 dozen cookies. Store in a tightly covered container.

Crunchy Milk & Wheat Germ Cookies ~ Omit the mint. Use chicken or beef stock or tomato juice instead of water if you like.

"There's just something about dogs that makes you feel good. You come home, they're thrilled to see you. They're good for the ego."
~Janet Schnellman

Crunchy Chicken
Parmesan Pretzels

Stocks are a great addition to dog cookies because they add flavour and protein. But try to use real broth instead of canned or bouillon cubes, which contain high quantities of salt and additives such as MSG.

2½ cups whole wheat flour
¼ cup skim milk powder
¼ cup Parmesan cheese
1 tsp. baking powder
1 cup chicken stock or water
2 tbsp. canola oil

"If you think dogs can't count, try putting three dog biscuits in your pocket and then giving Fido only two of them."
⁓Phil Pastoret

Buddy

Preheat oven to 375° F.

In a large bowl, combine flour, skim milk powder, Parmesan cheese, and baking powder. Add chicken stock and oil and stir until you have a stiff dough.

Pinch off walnut-sized pieces of dough, roll them into thin ropes, and shape the ropes into pretzels, pressing the ends to seal. You can make the pretzels as big or small as you like in order to suit the size of your dog, but increase the baking time accordingly. If you like, brush a little beaten egg over the tops of the pretzels and sprinkle with extra Parmesan or sesame seeds.

Bake for about 20 minutes, until firm. Turn off the oven but leave the pretzels inside for several hours to harden as they cool.

Makes about 2 dozen pretzels. Store in a tightly covered container.

Grrranola Pucks

If you like, omit the egg whites and serve the granola to your dog on its own. Resist the urge to add raisins, which can be toxic to dogs. Chopped dried apricots are fine though. To boost calcium, crumble the eggshells into the granola when you add the eggs.

2 cups oats
½ cup wheat germ or cracked wheat (bulgur)
½ cup chopped nuts and seeds (such as pecans, walnuts,
    almonds, pine nuts, or pumpkin and sunflower seeds)
Pinch cinnamon (optional)
Pinch salt
2 tbsp. canola oil
2 tbsp. honey or molasses
2 eggs

"My dog is usually pleased with what I do, because she is not infected with the concept of what I should be doing."
⁓Lonzo Idolswine

Preheat oven to 300° F.

In a large bowl, combine oats, wheat germ, nuts and seeds, cinnamon, and salt. Drizzle with oil and honey and toss well to coat.

Suki

Spread mixture on a rimmed baking sheet and bake for 20–30 minutes, stirring once or twice, until golden. Remove granola from the oven and set aside to cool.

Once the granola has cooled enough that it won't cook the eggs, stir the eggs into it. Divide the mixture between 12 muffin tins that have been sprayed with non-stick spray. Press each puck down with the back of a spoon. Bake for about 20 minutes, until golden and set. Let cool for 5–10 minutes, then remove them from the tins to cool completely.

Makes 1 dozen pucks. Store in a tightly sealed container.

Peanut Butter & Honey Cookies

It's no secret that dogs love peanut butter. It's also a great source of protein, vitamin E, niacin, folic acid, phosphorous, and magnesium. It's best to use natural peanut butter, which contains only peanuts—no sugar, salt, or additives.

Daisy

JULIE VAN ROSENDAAL

1 cup natural peanut butter
1 egg
2 tbsp. honey
¾ cup skim milk or water
2 cups whole wheat flour
1 tsp. baking powder

Preheat oven to 350° F.

In a large bowl, combine peanut butter, egg, honey, and milk. Add flour and baking powder and mix just until you have a soft dough.

Roll dough into walnut-sized balls and place 2" apart on a cookie sheet that has been sprayed with non-stick spray. Flatten each cookie with the back of a fork. If you like, sprinkle each cookie with some chopped peanuts and press a little to help them adhere.

Bake for about 15 minutes, until firm. Let them cool on the cookie sheet, or turn the oven off but leave them inside for several hours to harden as they cool.

Makes about 2 dozen cookies. Store in a tightly sealed container.

Peanut Butter, Oatmeal & Wheat Germ Cookies Replace one cup of flour with a cup of oats, and add $\frac{1}{4}$ cup wheat germ to the dry ingredients. Mix and bake as directed.

No-Bake Peanut Butter Carob Bites

Who wants to turn on the oven when it's hot outside? Mix up a batch of carob bites for your dog and some Rice Krispie treats for yourself, and take him for a run through the sprinkler.

½ cup carob powder
1 cup milk
½ cup natural peanut butter
2 tbsp. honey
1 tsp. vanilla
3 cups bran flakes

"No one appreciates the very special genius of
your conversation as the dog does."
~Christopher Morley

Boomer

In a large bowl, combine carob powder, milk, peanut butter, honey, and vanilla. Add bran flakes and mix well.

Roll into balls that suit the size of your dog, and refrigerate them for an hour or until firm.

Makes 2–3 dozen treats. Store in an airtight container in the fridge.

Peanut Butter Oatmeal Orbs

These bite-size snacks make perfect training treats. Keep a zip-lock bag of them in your pocket when you go for a walk.

1 cup whole wheat flour
2 cups oats
1 tsp. baking soda
¾ cup natural peanut butter
¾ cup water
2 tbsp. honey
1 egg
½ cup chopped unsalted peanuts, sunflower seeds,
    or carob chips

"When a man's dog turns against him, it is time for his wife to pack her trunk and go home to mamma."
~Mark Twain

Preheat oven to 350° F.

In a large bowl, stir together peanut butter, water, honey, and egg. Add flour, oats, and baking soda, and mix just until blended. Stir in peanuts, seeds, or carob chips.

Roll dough into small balls the size of large marbles and place on an ungreased baking sheet. Bake for about 10 minutes, until golden and firm.

Makes about 5 dozen treats. Store in a tightly sealed container.

Puppy Pancakes

These teeny pancakes are adorable, and perfect for puppies and older dogs who have difficulty with hard biscuits. If you like, stir half a cup of fresh blueberries or grated cheese into the batter. If you cook them in a pan after cooking ground beef or bacon, it will infuse the pancakes with the flavour of the meat.

1 cup whole wheat flour
¼ cup skim milk powder
1 tsp. baking powder
1 cup water
2 tbsp. canola oil
1 tbsp. honey
1 egg

"If a dog jumps in your lap, it is because he is fond of you;
but if a cat does the same thing, it is because your lap is warmer."
~Alfred North Whitehead

In a large bowl, combine flour, skim milk powder, and baking powder. In a small bowl, stir together water, oil, honey, and egg; add to the flour mixture and stir until blended.

Spray a large skillet with non-stick spray and place over medium heat. Drop spoonfuls of batter appropriate for the size of your dog onto the pan. Cook until bubbles rise to the surface and the bottoms are golden brown, about 2–4 minutes. Flip the pancakes and cook for another minute or two. Repeat with remaining batter. Cool before serving.

Makes about 1½ dozen 2"–3" pancakes. Store in a tightly sealed container or freeze.

Wheat Germ & Banana Pancakes ~ Stir 1 mashed ripe banana and ¼ cup wheat germ into the batter along with the wet ingredients. Cook as directed.

Apple Oatmeal Mini Muffins

Prepare a double batch of oatmeal the next time you make break-fast, and use the leftovers in these treats. Sunny Boy cereal works well too.

1½ cups whole wheat flour
¼ cup skim milk powder
1 tsp. baking powder
Pinch cinnamon
Pinch salt
1 cup cooked oatmeal, cooled
¾ cup water
1 egg
2 tbsp. canola oil
2 tbsp. honey
1 large apple, grated or chopped with the skin on

"Man is a dog's ideal of what God should be."
~Andre Malraux

Preheat oven to 350° F.

In a large bowl, combine flour, skim milk powder, baking powder, cinnamon, and salt. In a medium bowl, stir together oatmeal, water, egg, oil, and honey. Add to the dry ingredients along with the apple, and stir just until blended.

Spray mini muffin tins with non-stick spray and fill them with batter. Bake for 20–25 minutes, until the tops are springy to the touch.

Makes about 2½ dozen mini muffins. Store in a tightly sealed container, or freeze.

Peanut Butter & Banana Mini Muffins ~ Add 1 ripe banana, mashed or chopped, and ¼ cup natural peanut butter to the oatmeal mixture. Mix and bake as directed. These are great with a handful of bran or carob chips stirred in.

Rosemary Parmesan Twists

These are good enough for you to share with your dog ... but maybe you should learn a trick to earn one. It's only fair.

2½ cups whole wheat flour
½ cup grated Parmesan cheese
¼ cup fresh rosemary leaves—pull them off the twigs
Pinch salt
1 cup chicken stock or water
¼ cup canola or olive oil

Daisy Mae

In the bowl of a food processor, combine flour, Parmesan cheese, rosemary, and salt, and pulse until well blended. Pour the chicken stock and oil through the feed tube with the motor running and process until the dough forms a ball.

On a lightly floured surface, gently knead the dough about 10 times, or until smooth. Divide the dough in half; cover with a tea towel and let it rest for 15 minutes. Preheat the oven to 400° F.

On a lightly floured surface, roll each ball of dough into a 12" x 16" rectangle, and cut each into 2 dozen ½" wide strips. Twist each strip a few times and place on an ungreased cookie sheet.

Bake for about 10 minutes, until golden. Let them cool on the cookie sheet, or turn the oven off but leave them inside for several hours to harden.

Makes about 4 dozen twists. Store in a tightly covered container, or freeze.

Triple Cheese Bliss

This is what dogs dream about at night. No matter how many tricks they do in an attempt to get them, remember that treats should only make up about 10 per cent of your dog's diet; just like us, they can gain weight if they snack too much.

½ cup cottage cheese
½ cup grated cheddar cheese
½ cup Parmesan cheese
2 tbsp. canola oil
2 tbsp. water
1 egg, with or without the shell
1 clove garlic (optional)
2 cups whole wheat flour
Pinch salt

"You may have a dog that won't sit up, roll over or even cook breakfast, not because she's too stupid to learn how but because she's too smart to bother."
~Rick Horowitz, Chicago Tribune

Preheat oven to 350° F.

In the bowl of a food processor, combine all three cheeses, oil, water, egg, and garlic, and whiz until well blended. Add flour and salt, and pulse until the dough comes together. It may look crumbly, but it will be sticky and easy to shape.

Roll dough into walnut-sized balls and place 1" apart on a cookie sheet that has been sprayed with non-stick spray. Press them down with the back of a fork, like peanut butter cookies.

Bake for about 15 minutes, until firm. Let them cool on the cookie sheet, or turn the oven off but leave them inside for several hours to harden as they cool.

Makes about 2 dozen cookies. Store in a tightly sealed container, or freeze.

Cinnamon Rice Woofles

Barley is an excellent source of zinc, which is particularly important for northern breeds such as Siberian Huskies and Alaskan Malamutes, who have a genetic inability to adequately absorb zinc. Larger dogs are better suited to these treats, which are cooked in your waffle iron.

3 cups whole wheat flour
2 tsp. baking powder
1 tsp. cinnamon
1 cup cooked rice or barley, cooled
2 eggs
2 tbsp. canola oil
1¾ – 2 cups water, chicken stock, or skim milk

"In order to keep a true perspective of one's importance,
everyone should have a dog that will worship him
and a cat that will ignore him."
~Dereke Bruce

Hub

In a large bowl, combine flour, baking powder, and cinnamon. Add rice or barley, eggs, oil, and water and stir just until blended. Plug in your waffle iron to heat it up, and spray the surface with non-stick spray.

Spread as much batter as is appropriate for your waffle iron onto the hot surface. Close the lid and cook for about 5 minutes, until cooked through. Transfer to a wire rack to cool.

Makes about 5 large waffles, which should divide into 4 smaller waffles each. Store in a tightly covered container, or freeze.

Multigrain Molasses Cookies

Dogs require more calcium than humans do to counteract the high levels of phosphorous in meat. Skim milk powder and oats are both good sources. You can also stir finely crushed eggshells into your dog's cookies for a calcium boost.

2 cups whole wheat flour
½ cup oats
½ cup barley flakes
¼ cup wheat germ
¼ cup skim milk powder
Pinch cinnamon
Pinch salt
½ cup chicken stock or water
1 egg
2 tbsp. canola oil
2 tbsp. dark molasses
1 tsp. vanilla

Preheat oven to 350° F.

In a large bowl, combine flour, oats, barley flakes, wheat germ, skim milk powder, cinnamon, and salt. In a small bowl, stir together chicken stock, egg, oil, molasses, and vanilla. Add to the flour mixture and stir just until blended.

Roll dough into walnut-sized balls and place on a cookie sheet that has been sprayed with non-stick spray. Press down each cookie with the back of a fork, like peanut butter cookies.

Bake for about 15 minutes, until firm and golden around the edges. Let them cool on the cookie sheet or turn the oven off but leave them inside for several hours to harden as they cool.

Makes about 2 dozen cookies. Store in a tightly sealed container.

WALLY AEBLI

Dorian

Tomato & Cheese Cornmeal Twists

Experts have long recommended the use of tomato juice on animals who have found themselves on the wrong end of a skunk. Because tomatoes are highly acidic, the juice quickly neutralizes the skunk's strong, oily odours that get trapped in your pet's coat. Tomato juice is also a good source of antioxidants and vitamin C!

ANDREE-ANN THIVIERGE

Rex

2 cups whole wheat flour
1 cup grated cheddar cheese
½ cup cornmeal
¾ cup tomato juice
1 egg

Preheat oven to 325° F.

In a large bowl, combine flour, cheese, and cornmeal. Add tomato juice and egg and stir until you have a stiff dough.

Pinch off small balls of dough and roll them into thin ropes. Twist two ropes together and place on a cookie sheet that has been sprayed with non-stick spray.

Bake for about 20 minutes, until golden. Let them cool on the cookie sheet, or turn the oven off but leave them inside for several hours to harden as they cool.

Makes about 2 dozen twists. Store in a tightly covered container.

"Children and dogs are as necessary to the welfare of the country as Wall Street and the railroads."

~Harry S Truman

Molasses & Honey Braids

These are a little fancier and take more time than most cookies in this book, but are perfect if you want to package some special treats to give away as gifts. Buy inexpensive clear gift bags from the dollar store, or line new Chinese take-out boxes with coloured tissue and fill them with treats.

Molasses dough:
2 cups whole wheat flour
1 tsp. baking soda
½ tsp. cinnamon
¼ cup canola oil
¼ cup dark molasses
¼ cup water

Honey dough:
1½ cups all purpose flour
½ cup wheat germ or oat bran
1 tsp. baking soda
¼ cup canola oil
¼ cup honey
¼ cup water

"The average dog is a nicer person than the average person."
~Andrew A. Rooney

Preheat the oven to 350° F.

To make the molasses dough, combine flour, baking soda, and cinnamon in a large bowl. In a small bowl, stir together oil, molasses, and water. Add to the dry ingredients and stir just until you have a soft dough.

To make the honey dough, combine flour, wheat germ, and baking soda in a large bowl. In a small bowl, stir together the oil, honey, and water. Add to the dry ingredients and stir just until you have a soft dough.

To make the braids, pinch off 1" pieces of dough (or a size appropriate for your dog) and roll into ropes that are roughly the same length. Braid three ropes together, using opposing colors, or twist two ropes together, using one of each type, and place them on an ungreased cookie sheet.

Bake for about 20 minutes, until firm. Turn the oven off but leave the cookies inside for several hours or overnight to harden and cool.

Makes about 2 dozen braids.

Sundance

BROWNIES & BARS

Banana Carob Brownies

Besides being a great source of protein, eggs contain vitamin A, B vitamins, choline, essential fatty acids, and zinc. Bananas are packed with nutrients as well.

1 cup mashed bananas (about 2 bananas)
2 eggs
2 tbsp. canola oil
2 tbsp. honey
1 tsp. vanilla
1 cup whole wheat flour
¼ cup carob powder
1 tsp. baking powder
Pinch salt
¼ cup chopped walnuts (optional)

"My husband and I are either going to buy a dog or have a child. We can't decide whether to ruin our carpets or ruin our lives."
⁓Rita Rudner

Preheat oven to 350° F.

In a large bowl, combine bananas, eggs, oil, honey, and vanilla. In a small bowl, stir together the flour, carob powder, baking powder, and salt. Add to the banana mixture along with the walnuts, and stir just until combined.

Spread batter into an 8" x 8" pan that has been sprayed with non-stick spray. Bake for 30–35 minutes, until the top is springy to the touch. Cool in the pan.

Makes about 16 brownies. Store in a tightly sealed container, or freeze.

Carob Brownies

Human brownies are made with cocoa, which can be toxic to dogs, so carob is a better choice here. It also contains up to 80 per cent protein as well as magnesium, calcium, iron, phosphorus, potassium, and vitamins A, B, B2, B3, and D.

Brownies:
¼ cup canola oil
¼ cup honey
2 eggs
1 tsp. vanilla
1 cup flour
¼ cup carob powder
½ tsp. baking powder
½ cup carob chips or chopped walnuts (optional)

Carob Frosting:
1 – 8 oz. (250 g) pkg. light cream cheese
2 tbsp. carob powder
1 tbsp. honey

*"Every boy who has a dog should also have a mother,
so the dog can be fed regularly."*
~Anonymous

Preheat oven to 350° F.

In a large bowl, beat together oil, honey, eggs, and vanilla. Add flour, carob powder, and baking powder, and stir by hand just until combined. Gently stir in carob chips or walnuts.

Spread batter into an 8" x 8" pan that has been sprayed with non-stick spray. Bake for about 25 minutes, until top is springy to the touch. Cool in the pan or on a wire rack.

To make frosting, beat cream cheese, carob powder, and honey with enough water to make a spreadable frosting. You should need a couple spoonfuls. Wait until the brownies are completely cool before frosting.

Makes 16 brownies. Store extras in a tightly covered container, or freeze.

Carob Cheesecake Brownies ~ Omit frosting. In a small bowl, beat cream cheese and honey, omitting the carob powder, and drop in spoonfuls over the unbaked batter in the pan. Gently run the tip of a knife through both batters to create a swirled effect. Bake for 20–25 minutes, until the top is springy to the touch.

Baby Food Blondies

Make sure the baby food you buy doesn't contain onion powder; dogs often react to it, even when it's just a small amount.

1 cup cooked oatmeal or barley, cooled
¼ cup water or tomato juice
¼ cup skim milk powder
1 jar baby food beef, chicken, or turkey stew
1 egg
2 tbsp. canola oil
1 tbsp. honey
1½ cups whole wheat flour
1 tsp. baking powder
Pinch salt

"The world was conquered through the understanding of dogs; the world exists through the understanding of dogs."
~Nietzche

Judy

Preheat oven to 350° F.

In a large bowl, combine oatmeal, water, skim milk powder, baby food, eggs, oil, and honey. In a small bowl, stir together flour, baking powder, and salt. Add to the oatmeal mixture and stir just until blended.

Spread batter into a 9" x 13" pan that has been sprayed with nonstick spray. Bake for 25–30 minutes, until golden and springy to the touch. Cool in the pan.

Makes 2–3 dozen blondies.

Apple Apricot Blondies

Apricots contain the antioxidants lypocene and beta carotene, and are high in pectin, the natural fibre found in fruits. You can add a handful of chopped dried apricots as well if you like.

2 eggs
1 jar baby food apricots or peaches
¼ cup water
2 tbsp. canola oil
1 tbsp. honey
1 tsp. vanilla
1 cup whole wheat flour
¼ cup wheat germ
1 tsp. baking powder
Pinch salt
1 large apple, grated

"All knowledge, the totality of all questions and all answers is contained in the dog."
~Kafka

Preheat oven to 350° F.

In a large bowl, combine eggs, baby food, water, oil, honey, and vanilla. In a small bowl, stir together flour, wheat germ, baking powder, and salt. Add to the apricot mixture along with the apple, and stir just until blended.

Pour batter into an 8" x 8" pan that has been sprayed with non-stick spray. Bake for 30–35 minutes, until pale golden and springy to the touch. Cool in the pan.

Makes about 16 blondies.

Carrot Cake with Cream Cheese Frosting

If you want to make a birthday cake (or cupcakes) for your dog, this recipe is perfect. To make cupcakes, divide the batter into regular or mini muffin tins that have been sprayed with non-stick spray and bake at 400° F for 15–20 minutes, until springy to the touch.

Cake:
1 cup whole wheat flour
1 tsp. baking soda
¼ tsp. cinnamon
Pinch salt
½ cup applesauce
2 tbsp. canola oil
2 tbsp. honey
1 egg
1 tsp. vanilla
1 packed cup grated carrots (1 large or 2 medium carrots)
½ cup chopped walnuts (optional)

Cream Cheese Frosting (optional):
1 – 8 oz. (250g.) pkg. light cream cheese, softened
1 tbsp. honey

Preheat oven to 350° F.

In a large bowl, combine flour, baking soda, cinnamon, and salt. In a small bowl, stir together applesauce, oil, honey, egg, and vanilla. Add to the flour mixture along with the carrots and nuts and stir just until blended.

Spread batter in an 8" x 8" pan that has been sprayed with non-stick spray. Bake for 25–30 minutes, until springy to the touch. Cool in the pan.

To make frosting, beat cream cheese and honey until smooth, adding a little water as needed to achieve a spreadable consistency. Once completely cooled, spread carrot cake with frosting.

Makes 16–24 bars.

Fish Sticks

This is one of my most requested recipes—every dog I know goes absolutely mad for them. The omega-3 fatty acids found in tuna, salmon, and sardines are not considered as essential to dogs as they are to humans, but they are nutritionally beneficial in moderate amounts and have been shown to aid in the treatment of skin disease and arthritis.

2 cups oatmeal
1 cup cornmeal
1 tsp. dried parsley flakes (optional)
¼ tsp. baking powder
1 can tuna, salmon, or sardines (packed in water, undrained)
¼ cup water
2 tbsp. canola oil
1 egg
1 clove garlic, crushed

"Whoever said 'let sleeping dogs lie' didn't sleep with dogs."
~Unknown

Preheat oven to 350° F.

Place oatmeal in a food processor and whiz until coarsely ground. Add cornmeal, parsley flakes, and baking powder, and pulse to blend; transfer to a bowl and set aside. Place undrained tuna, salmon or sardines in the food processor with the water, oil, egg, and garlic, and whiz until well blended and almost smooth. Add to the oat mixture and stir just until combined.

Press the mixture into a 9" x 13" pan that has been sprayed with non-stick spray, and cut into 24 strips (6 widthwise by 4 length-wise) with a knife or pastry cutter.

Bake for 20–25 minutes, until golden and set. Let cool in the pan before separating into sticks.

Makes about 2 dozen fish sticks. Store in a tightly sealed container, or freeze.

MELISSA KEITH

Maggie

Liver Brownies

I know these sound delicious, but try to resist the temptation to eat them yourself. Liver is a great source of vitamin A, vitamin K, and the B vitamins.

SHERRILL LEWNEY

Ginger

1 lb. beef liver
¼ cup canola oil
2 tbsp. honey
2 eggs
1 cup whole wheat flour
½ tsp. baking powder
Pinch salt (optional)

"I'm a mog. Half man, half dog. I'm my own best friend."
~John Candy in Spaceballs

Preheat oven to 350° F.

Cut liver into chunks. In a food processor, blend the liver until it's liquefied, adding a little water if necessary. Add oil, honey, and eggs, and whiz until blended. Transfer to a large bowl.

Add flour, baking powder, and salt, and stir just until combined.

Spread batter in an 8" x 8" pan that has been sprayed with non-stick spray, and bake for 25–30 minutes, until the top is springy to the touch. (If you have a small dog, you can bake the brownies in a 9" x 13" pan for 15–20 minutes. This will make thinner brownies that can be cut into smaller squares.) Cool in the pan.

If you like, frost the cooled brownies with softened light cream cheese, sweetened with honey and thinned with a little water.

Makes about 16 brownies.

Peanut Butter & Banana Brownies

Bananas add flavour, moisture, sweetness, and potassium to dog treats. Overripe bananas are sweeter and more intensely flavoured than those that haven't ripened yet. If you have some but aren't ready to use them yet, throw them in the freezer whole, and thaw on the countertop or in a bowl of hot water when you're ready to bake.

1 cup mashed ripe bananas (about 2 bananas)
½ cup natural peanut butter
2 tbsp. canola oil
2 tbsp. honey
2 eggs
1 tsp. vanilla
1 cup whole wheat flour
1 tsp. baking powder
Pinch salt
¼ cup chopped unsalted peanuts (optional)

"The more I see of the representatives of the people,
the more I admire my dogs."
~Alphonse de Lamartine

Preheat oven to 350° F.

In a large bowl, combine bananas, peanut butter, oil, honey, eggs, and vanilla. Add flour, baking powder, salt, and peanuts, if using. Stir just until blended.

Spread batter in an 8" x 8" pan that has been sprayed with non-stick spray, and bake for 30–35 minutes, until the top is springy to the touch. (If you have a small dog, you can bake the brownies in a 9" x 13" pan for 15–20 minutes. This will make thinner brownies that can be cut into smaller squares.) Cool in the pan.

If you like, frost the cooled brownies with softened light cream cheese, sweetened with honey and thinned with a little water.

Makes about 16 brownies. Store in a tightly sealed container.

Oatmeal Molasses Nut Brownies

Oats are one of the best sources of complex carbohydrates to feed your dog. They are a source of protein, B complex vitamins, calcium, potassium, and magnesium. If you have an overripe banana, stir it in too.

1½ cups whole wheat flour
1 cup oatmeal
1 tsp. baking powder
Pinch salt
1 cup beef stock or milk
1 egg
2 tbsp. canola oil
2 tbsp. molasses
½ cup chopped walnuts

"I never married because I have three pets at home that answer the same purpose as a husband. I have a dog that growls every morning, a parrot that swears all afternoon, and a cat that comes home late at night."
~Marie Corelli

Preheat oven to 350° F.

In a large bowl, stir together flour, oatmeal, baking powder, and salt. In a medium bowl, stir together stock, egg, oil, and molasses. Add to the flour mixture along with the walnuts, and stir just until blended.

Pour into an 8" x 8" pan that has been sprayed with non-stick spray.

Bake for 25–30 minutes, until the top is springy to the touch. (If you have a small dog, you can bake the brownies in a 9" x 13" pan for 15–20 minutes. This will make thinner brownies that can be cut into smaller squares.) Cool in the pan.

Makes about 16 brownies.

Salad Bars

My dog would never touch any green vegetable . . . if he had beef stew, we would find all the peas licked clean at the bottom of the bowl when he was done. If yours is the same, omit the spinach! The double whammy of pumpkin and carrots gives these bars a huge boost of vitamin A in the form of beta carotene.

Bars:
1 cup whole wheat flour
1 tsp. baking powder
½ tsp. cinnamon
Pinch salt
2 eggs
½ cup canned pure pumpkin
¼ cup natural peanut butter
2 tbsp. tomato paste
2 tbsp. canola oil
1 tbsp. honey
1 tsp. vanilla
1 large carrot, grated
½ pkg (10 oz) frozen chopped spinach, thawed but not drained

Frosting (optional):
1 – 8 oz. (250 g) pkg. light cream cheese, softened
1 tbsp. honey

Preheat oven to 350° F.

In a large bowl, combine flour, baking powder, cinnamon, and salt. In a small bowl, stir together eggs, pumpkin, peanut butter, tomato paste, oil, honey, and vanilla. Add to the flour mixture along with the carrot and spinach, and stir just until combined.

Spread into an 8" x 8" pan that has been sprayed with non-stick spray. Bake for 25–30 minutes, until the top is springy to the touch. Cool in the pan.

To make frosting, beat cream cheese and honey until smooth. Spread over the bars once they have completely cooled.

Makes about 1 dozen bars.

"The dog is the god of frolic."
~Henry Ward Beecher

Cornbread

Because the lactose in buttermilk is already broken down, it won't cause problems if your dog is lactose intolerant. You can substitute thin plain yogurt if you don't have buttermilk.

1½ cups cornmeal
1 tsp. baking powder
1 tsp. baking soda
1 cup buttermilk
1 egg
2 tbsp. honey
2 tbsp. canola oil
½ cup whole kernel corn (optional)

"Outside of a dog, a book is probably man's best friend, and inside of a dog, it's too dark to read."

~Groucho Marx

Preheat oven to 350° F.

In a large bowl, combine cornmeal, baking powder, and baking soda. In a small bowl, whisk together buttermilk, egg, honey, and oil. Add to the cornmeal mixture, (along with the corn, if using), and stir just until blended.

Spread batter into an 8" x 8" pan that has been sprayed with non-stick spray. Bake for about 20 minutes, until golden and firm. Cool in the pan.

Makes about 16 squares. Store in a tightly covered container.

Bacon & Cheese Cornbread ~ Add a couple slices of cooked, crumbled bacon and ¼ cup grated cheddar cheese along with the corn, and use the bacon drippings in place of canola oil.

Blueberry Cornbread ~ Stir a cup of fresh or frozen blueberries into the batter before baking.

Chunky Apple Blondies

This blondie recipe lends itself well to many additions—blueberries, grated cheese and even grated carrot are all delicious. Or spread the cooled bars with natural peanut butter.

1½ cups whole wheat flour
½ tsp. baking powder
¼ tsp. cinnamon (optional)
Pinch salt (optional)
2 eggs
¼ cup honey
2 tbsp. canola oil
¼ cup applesauce
1 tsp. vanilla
2 apples, chopped or grated, with the skin left on

"Did you ever notice when you blow in a dog's face he gets mad at you? But when you take him in a car he sticks his head out the window."
∼Steve Bluestone

Hub

Preheat oven to 350 F.

In a large bowl, combine flour, cinnamon, baking powder, and salt. In a small bowl, stir together eggs, honey, oil, applesauce, and vanilla.

Add the egg mixture and chopped apple to the flour mixture and stir just until blended. Spread the batter into an 8" x 8" pan that has been sprayed with non-stick spray, and bake for about 30 minutes, until the top is springy to the touch. If you have a small dog, you can bake the brownies in a 9" x 13" pan for 15–20 minutes. This will make thinner brownies that can be cut into smaller squares. Cool in the pan.

Makes 16 brownies.

Apple Cheddar or Blueberry Blondies ~ Add ½ cup grated old cheddar, or fresh or frozen blueberries to the flour mixture along with the apples.

Apple Oatmeal Blondies ~ Add ½ cup oatmeal to the flour mixture. Bake as directed.

Daisy Mae

BISCOTTI

Molasses, Wheat Germ & Walnut Biscotti

While they don't replace tooth brushing, crunchy cookies contribute to good oral hygiene; their hard texture helps dogs maintain healthy teeth and gums.

2½ cups whole wheat flour
½ cup wheat germ
¼ cup skim milk powder
1 tsp. baking powder
Pinch cinnamon (optional)
¾ cup water
¼ cup molasses
1 egg
½ cup chopped walnuts (optional)

Preheat oven to 350° F.

In a large bowl, combine flour, wheat germ, skim milk powder, baking powder, and cinnamon. In a small bowl, stir together water, molasses, and egg. Add to the flour mixture along with the walnuts, and stir until well blended.

Shape the dough into a 12" long log, place on an ungreased baking sheet, and flatten until it's about 6" wide. If you like, brush the top with a little beaten egg to give it a shiny finish. Bake for about 30 minutes, until firm.

Reduce the oven temperature to 250° F. Cool the log and cut it on a slight diagonal into ½" thick slices using a sharp, serrated knife. Place the biscotti upright on the baking sheet, keeping them spaced about ½" apart, and put them back into the oven for another 30 minutes. If you want them hard, turn the oven off but leave them inside to harden as they cool.

Makes about 2 dozen biscotti. Store in a tightly covered container.

Banana, Oatmeal & Carob Chip Biscotti

To make an impressive gift, melt some extra carob chips and use them to dip or drizzle over the cooled biscotti.

1½ cups flour
1½ cups whole wheat flour
1 cup oats
1 tsp. baking powder
½ tsp. salt
Pinch cinnamon
⅓ cup water
1 ripe banana, mashed
1 egg
2 tbsp. canola oil
2 tbsp. honey
1 tsp. vanilla
½ cup carob chips

"My little dog—a heartbeat at my feet."
⁓Edith Wharton

Preheat oven to 350° F.

In a large bowl, combine both flours, oats, baking powder, salt, and cinnamon. In a small bowl, stir together water, banana, egg, oil, honey, and vanilla. Add to the flour mixture along with the carob chips, and stir until well blended.

Shape the dough into a log that is about 14" long, place on an ungreased baking sheet, and flatten until it's about 6" wide. If you like, brush the top with some beaten egg to give it a shiny finish. Bake for about 30 minutes, until firm.

Reduce the oven temperature to 250° F. Cool the log and cut it on a slight diagonal into ½" thick slices using a sharp, serrated knife. Place the biscotti upright on the baking sheet, keeping them spaced about ½" apart, and put them back into the oven for another 30 minutes. If you want them hard, turn the oven off but leave them inside to harden as they cool.

Makes about 2 dozen biscotti. Store in a tightly covered container.

Banana, Oatmeal & Blueberry Biscotti ~ Replace the carob chips with 1 cup fresh of frozen blueberries.

Oats & Honey Biscotti

To add even more flavour, replace the water with beef or chicken stock or tomato juice.

1½ cups flour
1½ cups whole wheat flour
1 cup oats
1 tsp. baking powder
Pinch salt (optional)
Pinch cinnamon (optional)
⅓ cup water
1 egg
2 tbsp. canola oil
3 tbsp. honey
1 tsp. vanilla

"I'd rather have an inch of a dog than miles of pedigree."
~Dana Burnet

Preheat oven to 350° F.

In a large bowl, combine flours, oats, baking powder, salt, and cinnamon. In a small bowl, stir together water, egg, oil, honey, and vanilla. Add to the dry ingredients and stir until blended.

Shape the dough into a log that is about 14" long, place on an ungreased baking sheet, and flatten until it's about 6" wide. If you like, brush the top with a little beaten egg to give it a shiny finish. Bake for about 30 minutes, until firm.

Reduce the oven temperature to 250° F. Cool the log and cut it on a slight diagonal into ½" thick slices using a sharp, serrated knife. Place the biscotti upright on the baking sheet, keeping them spaced about ½" apart, and put them back into the oven for another 30 minutes. If you want them hard, turn the oven off but leave them inside to harden as they cool.

Makes about 2 dozen biscotti. Store in a tightly covered container.

Oatmeal Carob Chip Biscotti ~ Add ½ cup carob chips to the dry ingredients along with the wet ingredients.

Cheese, Cornmeal & Garlic Biscotti

Linoleic acid, an omega-6 fatty acid, is essential in a dog's diet—dogs' bodies don't produce their own. Oils such as canola, sunflower, corn, and sesame are good sources of omega-6 fatty acids, which are important to maintain skin and coat health as well as reproductive function, and to boost the immune system. To fancy these biscotti up, stir in some chopped sun-dried tomatoes and basil.

1½ cups flour
1½ cups whole wheat flour
1 cup cornmeal
2 tbsp. dry skim milk powder
2 tsp. garlic powder
1 tsp. baking powder
1 cup chicken stock or water
¼ cup canola oil
1 egg
½ cup grated old cheddar cheese
¼ cup Parmesan cheese

Preheat oven to 350° F.

In a large bowl, combine flours, cornmeal, skim milk powder, garlic powder, and baking powder. In a small bowl, stir together chicken

Echo

stock, oil, and egg. Add to the dry ingredients along with the cheddar and Parmesan cheeses, and stir until well blended.

Shape the dough into a log that is about 14" long, place on an ungreased baking sheet, and flatten until it's about 6" wide. If you like, brush the top with a little beaten egg to give it a shiny finish. Bake for about 30 minutes, until firm.

Reduce the oven temperature to 250° F. Cool the log and cut it on a slight diagonal into ½" thick slices using a sharp, serrated knife. Place the biscotti upright on the baking sheet, keeping them spaced about ½" apart, and put them back into the oven for another 30 minutes. If you want them hard, turn the oven off but leave them inside to harden as they cool.

Makes about 2 dozen biscotti. Store in a tightly covered container.

Multigrain Apple Biscotti

Dogs need fibre too . . . it should comprise about 5 per cent of their diet. Older dogs require a well-balanced diet that is lower in calories, protein, and fat, and higher in fibre.

1 cup flour
2 cups whole wheat flour
1 cup cracked wheat (bulgur)
½ cup rye flour
½ cup cornmeal
¼ cup skim milk powder
Pinch salt
½ tsp. active dry yeast
¼ cup lukewarm water
1 cup chicken stock or water
1 apple, grated with the skin on
1 egg
2 tbsp. dark molasses or honey

Preheat oven to 350° F.

In a large bowl, combine flours, cracked wheat, rye flour, corn-meal, skim milk powder, and salt.

In a medium bowl, dissolve yeast in the water. Let it sit for a few minutes, until it gets foamy. Add the chicken stock, apple, egg, and molasses to the yeast mixture. Add to the dry ingredients and stir until you have stiff dough.

Divide the dough in half and shape each piece into an 8" x 3" log. Place the logs on an ungreased cookie sheet and flatten them so they are about 5" wide. If you like, brush the top with a little beaten egg to give it a shiny finish. Bake for about 30 minutes, until firm.

Reduce the oven temperature to 250° F. Cool the logs and cut them on a slight diagonal into ½" thick slices using a sharp, serrated knife. Place the biscotti upright on the baking sheet, keeping them spaced about ½" apart, and put them back into the oven for another 30 minutes. If you want them hard, turn the oven off but leave them inside to harden as they cool.

Makes about 2 dozen biscotti. Store in a tightly covered container.

Peanut Butter Biscotti with Milk & Honey

In addition to protein and fibre, peanuts and peanut butter also contain biotin, which is important for the metabolism of nutrients and maintenance of skin, fur, and nails.

1½ cups flour
1½ cups whole wheat flour
½ cup wheat germ or oat bran
1 tsp. baking powder
Pinch salt
1 egg
2 tbsp. canola oil
2 tbsp. honey
2 tbsp. skim milk powder
¾ cup water
¾ cup natural peanut butter
½ cup chopped peanuts or carob chips
  (optional)

"Money will buy a pretty good dog, but it won't buy the wag of his tail."
~Josh Billings

Preheat oven to 350° F.

In a large bowl, combine flours, wheat germ, baking powder, and salt. In a medium bowl, stir together egg, oil, honey, milk powder, and water. Add to the flour mixture along with the peanut butter and peanuts or carob chips, and stir until well blended.

Shape the dough into a log that is about 14" long, place on an ungreased baking sheet, and flatten until it's about 6" wide. If you like, brush the top with a little beaten egg to give it a shiny finish. Bake for about 30 minutes, until firm.

Reduce the oven temperature to 250° F. Cool the log and cut it on a slight diagonal into ½" thick slices using a sharp, serrated knife. Place the biscotti upright on the baking sheet, keeping them spaced about ½" apart, and put them back into the oven for another 30 minutes. If you want them hard, turn the oven off but leave them inside to harden as they cool.

Makes about 2 dozen biscotti. Store in a covered container.

Oatmeal Peanut Butter Biscotti ~ Replace the wheat germ with oatmeal. Roll the logs in a little dry oatmeal before baking, if you like.

Pumpkin Biscotti

You can cook and mash fresh pumpkin if you have an expired jack-o'-lantern around, but it's not necessarily worth the effort—canned pumpkin contains twenty times more beta carotene than fresh! If you do use fresh pumpkin, throw in some seeds as well to add protein, magnesium, iron, phosphorus, folic acid, and zinc.

2 cups whole wheat flour
1 cup flour
½ tsp. cinnamon
½ tsp. baking powder
1 cup canned pure pumpkin
¼ cup honey or molasses
2 tbsp. canola oil
1 egg
1 tsp. vanilla

"Happiness to a dog is what lies on the other side of a door."
~Charleton Ogburn Jr.

Preheat oven to 350° F.

In a large bowl, combine flours, cinnamon, and baking powder. In a small bowl, stir together pumpkin, honey, oil, egg, and vanilla. Add to the flour mixture and stir until well blended.

Shape the dough into a log that is about 14" long, place on an ungreased baking sheet, and flatten until it's about 6" wide. If you like, brush the top with a little beaten egg to give it a shiny finish. Bake for about 30 minutes, until firm.

Reduce the oven temperature to 250° F. Cool the log and cut it on a slight diagonal into ½" thick slices using a sharp, serrated knife. Place the biscotti upright on the baking sheet, keeping them spaced about ½" apart, and put them back into the oven for another 30 minutes. If you want them hard, turn the oven off but leave them inside to harden as they cool.

Makes about 2 dozen biscotti. Store in a tightly covered container.

Pumpkin Gingerbread Biscotti ~ Add ½ tsp. ground ginger along with the cinnamon, and replace the honey with molasses.

Beefy Biscotti

Beef is one of the best sources of protein for dogs, providing the amino acids necessary for healthy growth. Proteins from animal sources are preferable, as dogs have short digestive tracts and require easily digestible proteins.

2 cups whole wheat flour

½ cup wheat germ

2 tbsp. skim milk powder

½ cup beef stock, tomato juice, or water

¼ cup canola oil

1 egg

½ – 1 cup cooked lean ground beef,
    drained, or chopped leftover roast beef

Preheat oven to 350° F.

In a large bowl, combine flour, wheat germ, and skim milk powder. In a small bowl, stir together beef stock, oil, and egg. Add to the flour mixture along with the beef, and stir until well blended.

Shape the dough into a 12" long log, place on an ungreased baking sheet, and flatten until it's about 5" wide. If you like, brush the top with a little beaten egg to give it a shiny finish. Bake for about 30 minutes, until firm.

Reduce the oven temperature to 250° F. Cool the log and cut it on a slight diagonal into ½" thick slices using a sharp, serrated knife. Place the biscotti upright on the baking sheet, keeping them spaced about ½" apart, and put them back into the oven for another 30 minutes. If you want them hard, turn the oven off but leave them inside to harden as they cool.

Makes about 1½ dozen biscotti. Store in a tightly covered container in the fridge, or freeze.

Chicken or Sardine Biscotti ~ Replace the beef stock with chicken stock, and use chopped cooked chicken or a can of sardines, mashed with a fork, in place of the beef.

Pizza Biscotti

Tomatoes are a great source of vitamin C, which boosts immune system function.

2½ cups whole wheat flour
½ cup grated Parmesan cheese
½ cup cornmeal
1 clove garlic, crushed, or 1 tsp. garlic powder
1 tsp. dried basil, oregano, or Italian seasoning
Pinch salt
1 cup water or tomato juice
1 small can tomato paste
2 tbsp. olive or canola oil

"Our dogs wil love and admire the meanest of us, and feed our colossal vanity with their uncritical homage."
~Agnes Replier

In a large bowl, combine flour, Parmesan cheese, cornmeal, garlic, basil, oregano, and salt. Add water, tomato paste, and oil, and stir until well blended.

Sidney

Shape the dough into a log that is about 14" long, place on an ungreased baking sheet, and flatten until it's about 6" wide. If you like, brush the top with a little beaten egg to give it a shiny finish. Bake for about 30 minutes, until firm.

Reduce the oven temperature to 250° F. Cool the log and cut it on a slight diagonal into ½" thick slices using a sharp, serrated knife. Place the biscotti upright on the baking sheet, keeping them spaced about ½" apart, and put them back into the oven for another 30 minutes. If you want them hard, turn the oven off but leave them inside to harden as they cool.

Makes about 2 dozen biscotti. Store in a tightly covered container.

Carrot Biscotti

If you want, you could use this dough to roll out and cut into shapes. Or roll it into balls as small as you like, flatten them with a fork as if you were making peanut butter cookies, and bake them until they are firm.

4–5 large carrots, scrubbed and cut into chunks
2 eggs
2 cloves garlic, crushed
1 tbsp. honey
2 cups whole wheat flour
1 cup oats
¼ cup wheat germ
Pinch cinnamon (optional)

JANET & RICK HUGHES

Echo

"Dogs' lives are too short. Their only fault, really."
~Agnes Sligh Turnbull

Preheat oven to 350° F.

Bring an inch of water to a simmer in a medium saucepan. Add the carrots, cover, and cook until very soft. Drain, reserving the liquid, and mash the carrots. You should have about 2 cups. Pour about ¼ cup of the reserved carrot liquid over the oats and set them aside for about 10 minutes.

Put the carrots in a bowl, and stir in the eggs and garlic. Add the oats, flour, wheat germ, and cinnamon, and stir until well blended.

Shape the dough into a 12" long log, place on an ungreased baking sheet and flatten until it's about 6" wide. You can also brush the top with a little beaten egg to give it a shiny finish. Bake for about 30 minutes, until firm.

Reduce the oven temperature to 250° F. Cool the log and cut it on a slight diagonal into ½" thick slices using a sharp, serrated knife. Place the biscotti upright on the baking sheet, keeping them spaced about ½" apart, and put them back into the oven for another 30 minutes. If you want them hard, turn the oven off but leave them inside for several hours or overnight to harden as they cool.

Makes about 2 dozen biscotti. Store in a tightly covered container.

Notes

"Whoever said you can't buy happiness forgot little puppies."
~Gene Hill

Notes

"My dog is worried about the economy because Alpo is up
to 99 cents a can. That's almost $7.00 in dog money."
~Joe Weinstein

JULIE VAN ROSENDAAL is the author of the bestselling cookbooks *One Smart Cookie* and *Grazing* and is in demand to teach classes, appear on TV and radio, speak to various groups, and demonstrate her culinary wizardry at events and benefits across North America. She is also a regular contributor to newspapers and she has been featured in such publications as *Shape*, *Prevention* and *Woman's World* magazines. When she isn't travelling, Julie divides her time between Vancouver and Calgary, where she is working on what is sure to be her next bestselling cookbook.